THE FORGOTTEN FOUR

Breaking the Color Barrier in Pro Football

Elliott Smith
Cicely Lewis, Executive Editor

Lerner Publications ◆ Minneapolis

LETTER FROM CICELY LEWIS

Dear Reader,

When you think of today's star Black athletes, who comes to mind? Maybe you think of LeBron James, Mookie Betts, Dak Prescott, or Simone Biles. They are all great athletes. But do you know who paved the way for them?

Cicely Lewis

I began Read Woke Books to challenge social norms and to share stories of people from underrepresented and oppressed groups. In this series, you will be introduced to lesser-known athletes and the barriers they overcame to make great changes in sports.

Sports is more than a game. Throughout history, sports have been a way to help fight injustices in our world. As you read, think about how the actions athletes have made in their sports have impacted the world.

I hope these books inspire you to never give up. Someone has to take the first step, and it might as well be you.

Power to the Reader,

Cicely Lewis, Executive Editor

TABLE OF CONTENTS

Wide receiver Bobby Mitchell catches a pass before making a touchdown during a 1967 game.

THE FINAL STEP

Much of the US was segregated for decades. Laws forbade Black people from using the same places as white people, such as schools. Sports were segregated too. But by 1955, only one team in the National Football League (NFL) had not integrated.

The Washington Redskins were owned by George Preston Marshall, a white man. Even though his team struggled to win games, he refused to add Black players.

In 1961 the federal government had enough. They refused

to let Washington play in their new stadium until the team integrated. Marshall had no choice. Before the 1962 season, he traded for wide receiver Bobby Mitchell.

Mitchell's first game with Washington was one to remember. He weaved through the Dallas Cowboys defense for a 92-yard kickoff return touchdown. He later joined the Pro Football Hall of Fame in 1983. Like many of the people in this book, his impact and courage are part of the proud legacy of Black people in football.

Mitchell (*shown in 1962*) played four seasons with the Cleveland Browns and seven seasons with Washington.

IMPORTANT NOTE: The Washington Redskins were renamed the Washington Commanders in 2022. *Redskin* is an offensive term for Native Americans.

Thousands of people attend a college football game at the Los Angeles Coliseum in 1945.

CHAPTER 1

BREAKING BARRIERS

The American Professional Football Association formed in 1920 with 10 teams and added four more later that year. Before the 1922 season, it was renamed the NFL. The NFL featured a few Black players in the early years. But in 1933, white NFL owners changed course. In an informal agreement, they banned Black players from the league.

Without a pro league to play in, many of the best Black college football players stopped playing. The owners' agreement remained in place until 1946. It might have stayed that way longer if not for the efforts of several key people.

In 1946 the Cleveland Rams decided to move to Los Angeles, California. They planned to use the Los Angeles Coliseum as their stadium. This drew the attention of Black journalist Halley Harding. He spoke at a meeting with the stadium's leaders and argued why the Rams could not play there unless the team integrated.

Kenny Washington of the Los Angeles Rams catches a pass made by the opposing team during a 1948 game.

DID YOU KNOW?

In 1919 Fritz Pollard became the first Black player to join the American Professional Football Association. Two years later, he became the first Black coach in the NFL.

Halfback Fritz Pollard of the Brown University Brown Bears in 1916

Harding also suggested Kenny Washington as a Rams player. Washington was a local football star from the University of California, Los Angeles (UCLA). White stadium leader Roger Jessup agreed with Harding. He told the Rams general manager that if Washington couldn't play for the Rams, the team would not be welcome at the Coliseum.

(*Back row, left to right*) Kenny Washington, Bob Waterfield, (*front row, left to right*) Jack Finlay, Nate de Francisco, and Woody Strode of the Los Angeles Rams in 1946

In March 1946, the Rams signed Washington. Later that year, they signed Washington's UCLA teammate Woody Strode. The Cleveland Browns signed Marion Motley and Bill Willis.

Washington, Strode, Motley, and Willis became known as the Forgotten Four. They helped integrate pro football and opened the door for other Black players in the NFL.

Cleveland Browns players (*back row, left to right*) Bill Willis, Frank Gatski, George Young, Mac Speedie, Lin Houston, (*front row, left to right*) Dante Lavelli, Marion Motley, Lou Groza, and Otto Graham in 1952

Woody Strode in 1946

REFLECT

Many football fans are unfamiliar with the Forgotten Four even though the NFL is the most popular sports league in the US. How could this be changed? Why is this important?

Safety Rosey Taylor of the Chicago Bears returning a kick in the 1960s

CHAPTER 2
QUARTERBACK QUEST

Even after the NFL began adding Black players, many coaches only considered white players for some positions. Coaches gave Black players positions such as running back or wide receiver. But racist thinking and stereotypes prevented them from putting Black players in positions such as quarterback.

Quarterback is one of the most important positions in the game. The quarterback must think quickly and be a leader to the team. Some coaches in the league thought that white players were smarter than Black players and would be better as quarterbacks.

Players also had to take the Wonderlic test. Coaches used the fifty-question test to predict a player's success in the NFL. But people have argued the test is racially biased against Black players. And it was never proven that high Wonderlic test scores meant players would perform better in the NFL. The NFL used the test until 2022.

Fullback Jim Brown makes a touchdown in a 1960 game.

REFLECT

Some NFL coaches refused to let Black players be quarterbacks for many years. What does this say about those coaches in the league? How does this impact the league and its players? How might the league make this better?

This test and racist thinking meant many Black college quarterbacks were forced to switch positions when entering the NFL. Those who refused to switch often went undrafted. Some ended up playing in the Canadian Football League.

In 1968 Marlin Briscoe became the first Black quarterback to start in the NFL. Briscoe was a quarterback in college, but the Denver Broncos drafted him as a cornerback. It took three other quarterbacks to get injured or benched before Briscoe got his chance.

DID YOU KNOW?

In 1968 Eldridge Dickey became the first Black quarterback picked in the first round of the American Football League's draft. The American Football League formed in 1960 and merged with the NFL in 1970.

Marlin Briscoe (*number 15*) playing for the Denver Broncos in 1968

Briscoe's shot at quarterback was short-lived. The Broncos let him go the next season. He played wide receiver in the last years of his NFL career. Other Black quarterbacks such as Eldridge Dickey and Joe Gilliam got few or no chances to play.

DID YOU KNOW?

The 2023 Super Bowl was the first big game to feature two Black starting quarterbacks. Patrick Mahomes of the Kansas City Chiefs defeated Jalen Hurts of the Philadelphia Eagles.

In 1978 Doug Williams became the first Black NFL quarterback drafted in the first round. Ten years later, he became the first Black quarterback to start and win a Super Bowl.

Quarterback Doug Williams celebrates winning the Super Bowl in 1988.

The thinking around Black quarterbacks has changed over time. More are making an impact in the league. In 2023 quarterbacks Bryce Young, C. J. Stroud, and Anthony Richardson were chosen in the first round of the NFL Draft.

Quarterback Bryce Young holds up his Carolina Panthers jersey after being picked in the 2023 NFL Draft.

"It's not black quarterback anymore, just quarterback. They're judged on the merits of their ability—or lack thereof, which is an accomplishment I'm glad to see while I'm on this earth."

—Marlin Briscoe, former quarterback, 2014

Los Angeles Raiders head coach Art Shell before opening kickoff on October 9, 1989

CHAPTER 3

SIDELINE PROGRESS

In 2022 Black players made up nearly 60 percent of the NFL. But Black coaches were rare on NFL sidelines for a long time. In 1980 only 14 out of 262 assistant coaches were Black. No head coaches were Black.

Art Shell became head coach of the Los Angeles Raiders in 1989. He was the league's first Black head coach. Shell led the Raiders to an 8–8 record his first season and a 12–4 record the next season.

Even with Shell's success, there have been few Black head

coaches. There have been more than 500 head coaches since the NFL began in 1920. Only 25 have been Black. That's a very low number for a league mainly made up of Black players.

In 2003 the NFL started the Rooney Rule. The rule is named after the former leader of the NFL's diversity group, Dan Rooney of the Pittsburgh Steelers. It requires teams to interview people from underrepresented backgrounds for coaching jobs. Some people say the rule doesn't work. They argue that teams simply use a person from an underrepresented background to fill a slot when they already have their choice made.

Black coaches including Jim Caldwell and Brian Flores have been fired after winning seasons, while non-Black coaches

Detroit Lions head coach Jim Caldwell during a 2014 game

continue working after worse seasons. Flores sued the NFL in 2022, claiming the NFL was racist in its hiring. Two other Black coaches joined Flores in suing.

"The Rooney rule is intended to give minorities the opportunity to sit down in front of ownership. But I think what it's turned into is an instance where guys are just checking the box."

—Brian Flores, former Miami Dolphins coach, 2022

Miami Dolphins head coach Brian Flores speaks to the referee and down judge during a 2021 game.

REFLECT

How can the NFL improve Black candidates' chances to become head coaches? Why is this important?

For years, the situation for other NFL jobs wasn't much better. In 2002 Ozzie Newsome of the Baltimore Ravens became the first Black general manager. There were eight Black general managers and five Black team presidents beginning the 2023 season. These were major gains for Black people in the league.

Sandra Douglass Morgan, president of the Las Vegas Raiders, in 2022

Left to right: San Francisco 49ers players Eli Harold, Colin Kaepernick, and Eric Reid kneel during the national anthem before a 2016 game.

CHAPTER 4

LEGACY OF CHANGE

People continue to break barriers in the NFL. Colin Kaepernick played a huge role in recent NFL history. In 2016 the former San Francisco 49ers quarterback sat and then later kneeled during the national anthem at NFL games. People often stand during the anthem to honor the US.

By kneeling, Kaepernick was protesting injustice and police brutality. He was calling on the US to be a better, fairer place for all Americans. But some people viewed his kneeling during the anthem as a sign that he didn't support the country.

Some players joined Kaepernick in kneeling. Some fans protested outside of stadiums. Kaepernick's kneeling helped to raise awareness of racial injustice at a time when people around the country were facing the issue.

Kaepernick ended his contract with the 49ers after the 2016 season. He moved into working for social change. As of 2023, he still trained and hoped to play for another NFL team.

Many Black players were upset in 2020 after a police officer murdered George Floyd in Minneapolis, Minnesota. They hoped the league and teams would make statements

In 2020 members of the Minnesota Vikings kneel during the national anthem.

against police brutality. But few did. So Saquon Barkley, Patrick Mahomes, and other players made a video in which they asked the league to condemn racism and police brutality.

The NFL said it needed to do better. Players can add messages such as Black Lives Matter to the backs of their helmets. And the league and its teams have donated more than $250 million to fight racism.

A Black Lives Matter sticker as seen on quarterback Geno Smith's helmet

REFLECT

NFL players are using their platform to tell fans and owners that Black Lives Matter. Why do you think it's important for Black players to speak out? What are some ways that you can make a difference in your community?

DID YOU KNOW?

Collette Smith became the first Black female NFL coach in 2017. In 2023 Autumn Lockwood became the first Black woman to coach in a Super Bowl.

Things are also changing on the sidelines. In 2021 Jennifer King of the Washington Commanders became the first Black woman to hold a full-time coaching position in the league. That year Maia Chaka became the first Black woman to referee in an NFL game.

Line judge Maia Chaka during a 2021 game

"Sports has kind of always been my thing, and it was big in my family as well. I just kind of developed a really big love for it at a young age. Love to play it, love to watch it. And now I get to coach it."

—Jennifer King, Washington Commanders coach, 2021

Washington Commanders running backs coach Jennifer King leads a warmup before a game in 2022.

Mellody Hobson speaks at the UCHealth Training Center in 2022.

In 2022 Mellody Hobson joined ownership of the Denver Broncos. It made her the first Black woman to own part of an NFL team.

Football is America's most popular sport. From the Forgotten Four to ownership, Black people have played an important role in the NFL's rise. And their role will continue.

GLOSSARY

barrier: something that blocks or prevents a person from doing something

bias: a prejudice that favors or works against a person or group of people

condemn: to call something wrong or to strongly disapprove

draft: a yearly event where teams take turns choosing new players

general manager: the person in a football front office who controls all player-related decisions

injustice: an act that is wrong or not fair

integrate: to make a place or job open to all racial and ethnic groups

police brutality: the excessive or illegal use of force of law enforcement against a person or group

segregate: the practice of separating people based on race

stereotype: an idea of what someone will do, say, or think based on what groups they belong to, such as racial groups

SOURCE NOTES

17 Billy Witz, "A Pioneering Black Quarterback's Lasting Legacy," *New York Times*, January 29, 2014, https://www.nytimes.com/2014/01/30/sports/football/a-pioneering-black-quarterbacks-lasting-legacy.html.

20 Elisha Fieldstadt, "Brian Flores Says His Giants Interview Was for Show to Satisfy 'Rooney Rule,'" ABC News, updated February 3, 2022, https://www.nbcnews.com/news/us-news/brian-flores-says-giants-interview-was-show-satisfy-rooney-rule-rcna14529.

26 Senita Brooks, "A King among Kings," *Sports Illustrated*, November 5, 2021, https://www.si.com/nfl/2021/11/05/jennifer-king-washington-football-team-coach-100-influential-black-women.

READ WOKE READING LIST

Britannica Kids: Colin Kaepernick
https://kids.britannica.com/students/article/Colin-Kaepernick/632842

Britannica Kids: National Football League (NFL)
https://kids.britannica.com/students/article/National-Football-League-NFL/624440

Flynn, Brendan. *The NFL Encyclopedia*. Minneapolis: Abdo Reference, 2022.

Hoena, Blake. *Colin Kaepernick: Athletes Who Made a Difference*. Minneapolis: Graphic Universe, 2020.

Kiddle: Bobby Mitchell Facts for Kids
https://kids.kiddle.co/Bobby_Mitchell

Smith, Elliott. *Black Achievements in Sports: Celebrating Fritz Pollard, Simone Biles, and More*. Minneapolis: Lerner Publications, 2024.

Sports Illustrated Kids: The Untold Story of the Integration of Pro Football
https://www.sikids.com/kid-reporter/forgotten-four-who-integrated-nfl

USA Today: A Brief History of Black NFL Coaches
https://www.usatoday.com/storytelling/graphic-novels/sports/nfl/history-nfl-black-coaches/1663620921633/

INDEX

PHOTO ACKNOWLEDGMENTS

Images: Bettmann/Getty Images, pp. 4, 16; AP Photo, pp. 5, 9, 10, 11, 13; AP Photo/Harold P. Matosian, p. 6; AP Photo/Pro Football Hall of Fame, pp. 7, 8; AP Photo/Vernon Biever, p. 12; Carl Iwasaki/Sports Illustrated/Getty Images, p. 15; David Eulitt/Getty Images, p. 17; AP Photo/Mark Lennihan, p. 18; Jeff Haynes/AP Images for Panin, p. 19; AP Photo/Fred Kfoury III/Icon Sportswire, p. 20; Ethan Miller/Getty Images, p. 21; AP Photo/Marcio Jose Sanchez, p. 22; AP Photo/David Berding, p. 23; Amy Lemus/NurPhoto/Getty Images, p. 24; AP Photo/Logan Bowles, p. 25; AP Photo/Kevin Terrell, p. 26; Hyoung Chang/The Denver Post/Getty Images, p. 27. Design elements: Sandipkumar Patel/Getty Images; Colors Hunter/Getty Images. Cicely Lewis portrait photos by Fernando Decillis.

Cover: AP Photo; AP Photo/Pro Football Hall of Fame.

Lerner Publications Company
An imprint of Lerner Publishing Group, Inc.
241 First Avenue North
Minneapolis, MN 55401 USA

For reading levels and more information, look up this title at www.lernerbooks.com.

Main body text set in Aptifer Sans LT Pro.
Typeface provided by Linotype AG.

Editor: Brianna Kaiser **Designer:** Viet Chu
Lerner team: Martha Kranes

Library of Congress Cataloging-in-Publication Data

Names: Smith, Elliott, 1976– author.
Title: The forgotten four : breaking the color barrier in pro football / Elliott Smith.
Description: Minneapolis, MN : Lerner Publications, [2025] | Series: Black trailblazers in sports (read woke books) | Includes bibliographical references and index. | Audience: Ages 9–14 | Audience: Grades 4–6 | Summary: "Millions of people watch the NFL every year, but Black men weren't always allowed to play. Learn about the NFL's beginning, football's Forgotten Four, and football players' ongoing fight for racial justice"— Provided by publisher.
Identifiers: LCCN 2023034486 (print) | LCCN 2023034487 (ebook) | ISBN 9798765611562 (library binding) | ISBN 9798765628508 (paperback) | ISBN 9798765632802 (epub)
Subjects: LCSH: Football—United States—History. | African American football players. | National Football League. | Racism in sports—United States. | United States—Race relations.
Classification: LCC GV950 .S65 2025 (print) | LCC GV950 (ebook) | DDC 796.332—dc23/eng/20230803

LC record available at https://lccn.loc.gov/2023034486
LC ebook record available at https://lccn.loc.gov/2023034487

Manufactured in the United States of America
1-1010006-51778-12/13/2023